CONTENTS

	Page
Session # 1: Assurance of Salvation	1
Session # 2: Baptism	5
Session # 3: Prayer	8
Session # 4: Bible Study & Devotions	12
Session # 5: Your Faith Story	16
Session # 6: God's Story—THE BRIDGE	21
Session # 7: Church: Christian Community	25
Session # 8: Practice Being the Church	29
Memory Verses	32

I0190390

ACKNOWLEDGEMENTS

Many of the ideas contained in this study are adapted from Ying Kai and T4T (Training for Trainers) that Ying developed in his work overseas in which nearly 5 million people have been saved. Many thanks also to Gary Stump, pastor of Onward Church in Fishers, IN for contextualizing the American version of T4T.

(Edition Revised September 2019)

TRANSFORMING CHURCHES NETWORK

Transforming Churches Network
1736 Edgeburg Lane
Cordova, TN 38016
901-494-7375
www.tcnprocess.com
terry@transformingchurchesnetwork.org

<u>Session 1—Assurance of Salvation</u>

INTRODUCTION: This discipleship training is to be done either one-on-one or in small groups where one person is discipling the other(s).

> **NOTE** These note boxes contain important information. Be sure to read each "NOTE" out loud during your time together.

☐ BEGIN BY PRAYING TOGETHER

☐ LIST A HIGHLIGHT FROM LAST WEEK & CHALLENGE YOU ARE FACING

Highlight   Challenge

_____   _____

_____   _____

☐ WHAT IS YOUR SPIRITUAL CONDITION?

Romans 10:9 (NLT) If you confess with your mouth that Jesus is Lord and believe in your heart that God raised him from the dead, you will be saved.

Have you confessed Jesus as your Lord?
☐ Yes   ☐ No   ☐ I'm Not Sure

Do you believe in your heart God raised Him from the dead?
☐ Yes   ☐ No   ☐ I'm Not Sure

If you answered "yes" to both questions, what does this passage say

is your condition? _____

☐ READ AND DISCUSS EACH SCRIPTURE BELOW:

> **NOTE** The Purpose of this Session is to help you understand what happened to you when you confessed your faith in Jesus. Here are Bible verses to help you understand and be certain of your new relationship in Christ.

1) **John 1:12 (NKJV) But as many as received Him, to them He gave the right to become children of God, to those who believe in His name.**

   What makes you a child of God?

2) **Acts 16:31 (NKJV) So they said, "Believe on the Lord Jesus Christ, and you will be saved, you and your household."**

   When the Bible says saved, what are you saved from?

3) **Romans 3:28 (NIV84) For we maintain that a man is justified by faith apart from observing the law.**

   What causes you to be "justified?" (Justified means that you are no longer under the penalty of your sin.)

4) **Romans 4:5 (NLT) But people are counted as righteous, not because of their work, but because of their faith in God who forgives sinners.**

   What causes you to be counted as righteous before God?

5) **Ephesians 2:8–9 (NIV84) For it is by grace you have been saved, through faith—and this not from yourselves, it is the gift of God—not by works, so that no one can boast.**

   What can't you do because you have been saved by grace through faith?

6) *John 5:24 (NIV84) "I tell you the truth, whoever hears my word and believes him who sent me has eternal life and will not be condemned; he has crossed over from death to life."*

As a believer, what can never happen to you?

7) *John 10:27–29 (NLT) "My sheep listen to my voice; I know them, and they follow me. [28] I give them eternal life, and they will never perish. No one can snatch them away from me, [29] for my Father has given them to me, and he is more powerful than anyone else. No one can snatch them from the Father's hand."*

How secure are you in God's hand?

8) *Romans 8:38–39 (NLT) And I am convinced that nothing can ever separate us from God's love. Neither death nor life, neither angels nor demons, neither our fears for today nor our worries about tomorrow—not even the powers of hell can separate us from God's love. [39] No power in the sky above or in the earth below—indeed, nothing in all creation will ever be able to separate us from the love of God that is revealed in Christ Jesus our Lord.*

From what can you never be separated?

9) *1 John 5:11–13 (NIV84) And this is the testimony: God has given us eternal life, and this life is in his Son. [12] He who has the Son has life; he who does not have the Son of God does not have life. [13] I write these things to you who believe in the name of the Son of God so that you may know that you have eternal life.*

Do you know whether or not you have eternal life? Is your salvation secure?

☐ Yes　　　　☐ No　　　　☐ I'm Not Sure

ASSIGNMENT FOR NEXT TIME:

1. READ: Begin reading the Gospel of John before the next session.

Why should you start with the Gospel of John? Because of the purpose of the Gospel of John:

John 20:30–31 (NLT) The disciples saw Jesus do many other miraculous signs in addition to the ones recorded in this book. But these are written so that you may continue to believe that Jesus is the Messiah, the Son of God, and that by believing in him you will have life by the power of his name.

Read one chapter per day for the purpose of getting to know Jesus better and growing in your faith.

2. MEMORIZE this Bible verse:

MEMORIZE

> *Romans 10:9 (NLT) If you confess with your mouth that Jesus is Lord and believe in your heart that God raised him from the dead, you will be saved.*

NOTE

> In the back of this booklet you will find the **Memory Verse** for each session. You can cut them out and carry them with you as you memorize the Bible verse each week.

☐ CLOSE IN PRAYER TOGETHER

Session 2—Baptism

☐ BEGIN BY PRAYING TOGETHER

☐ LIST A HIGHLIGHT FROM LAST WEEK & CHALLENGE YOU ARE FACING

Highlight   Challenge

_____   _____

_____   _____

☐ HOW ARE YOU DOING READING THE GOSPEL OF JOHN?
What is something you learned about the Lord?
What questions do you have from what you have read?

☐ DID YOU MEMORIZE ROMANS 10:9? IF SO, CAN YOU SHARE IT?

> **NOTE** The next step after trusting in Jesus for a new believer is to be baptized according to Jesus' command. This Session will explain the reasons and benefits of baptism.

☐ READ THE FOLLOWING BIBLE VERSES & ANSWER THE QUESTIONS:

1) *Matthew 28:19-20 (NIV) Go and make disciples of all nations, baptizing them in the name of the Father and of the Son and of the Holy Spirit, and teaching them to obey everything I have commanded you.*

   Who commanded baptism?

   When was the command given?

   Who should be baptized?

2) *Acts 2:38-39 (NIV) Repent and be baptized, every one of you, in the name of Jesus Christ for the forgiveness of your sins.*

3) *Romans 6:4 (NLT) For we died and were buried with Christ by baptism. And just as Christ was raised from the dead by the glorious power of the Father, now we also may live new lives.*

4) **1 Peter 3:21 (NIV) This water (of Noah's flood) symbolizes baptism that now save you also...It saves you by the resurrection of Jesus Christ.**

What benefits does baptism give?

1)

2)

3)

5) **Mark 16:16 (NIV) Whoever believes and is baptized will be saved, but whoever does not believe will be condemned.**

To whom does baptism give all these blessings?

WHAT ABOUT CHILDREN AND BABIES? THEY SHOULD ALSO BE BAPTIZED BECAUSE:

A) THEY ARE INCLUDED IN THE WORDS "ALL NATIONS";

Matthew 28:19-20 (NIV) Go and make disciples of all nations, baptizing them in the name of the Father and of the Son and of the Holy Spirit.

B) AS SINNERS, THEY NEED WHAT BAPTISM OFFERS;

John 3:5-6 (NIV) No one can enter the kingdom of God unless he is born of water and the Spirit. Flesh gives birth to flesh, but the Spirit gives birth to spirit.

C) THEY ARE ALSO ABLE TO HAVE FAITH.

Matthew 18:6 (NIV) If anyone causes one of these little ones who believe in Me to sin, it would be better for him to have a large millstone hung around his neck and to be drowned in the depths of the sea.

HOW CAN WATER DO SUCH GREAT THINGS?

It is not just the water, but the word of God in and with the water that does these things, along with faith, which trusts this word of God in the water. Baptism then, is, a life-giving water connected to God's word, rich in grace, and a washing of the new birth in the Holy Spirit.

6) Titus 3:5-8 (N(V) *He saved us through the washing of rebirth and renewal by the Holy Spirit, whom He poured out on us generously through Jesus Christ our Savior, so that, having been justified by His grace, we might become heirs having the hope of eternal life. This is a trustworthy saying.*

Why should you be baptized? (check all that apply)
☐ Jesus commanded us to be baptized.
☐ I need and want all of the great blessings it offers.
☐ It illustrates what it means to die to my old life, and to live a new life with Jesus

When were you baptized? (check one)
☐ I have never been baptized
☐ I was baptized as a child
☐ I was baptized, but not in the Name of the Father, Son & Holy Spirit
☐ Other:

Explain: _____

If you are hesitating about being baptized, why? (check all that apply)
☐ I don't understand baptism.
☐ I don't believe it is necessary.
☐ I'm simply afraid or embarrassed.

ASSIGNMENT FOR NEXT TIME:

1. Continuing reading the Gospel of John. Read it more than once.

2. Schedule your baptism.

MEMORIZE

Acts 22:16 (NLT) 'What are you waiting for? Get up and be baptized. Have your sins washed away by calling on the name of the Lord.'

☐ CLOSE IN PRAYER TOGETHER

<u>Session 3—Prayer</u>

☐ BEGIN BY PRAYING TOGETHER

☐ LIST A HIGHLIGHT FROM LAST WEEK & CHALLENGE YOU ARE FACING

Highlight	Challenge
_____	_____
_____	_____

☐ DESCRIBE YOUR PROGRESS IN READING THE GOSPEL OF JOHN?

☐ DID YOU MEMORIZE ACTS 22:16? IF SO, CAN YOU SHARE IT?

☐ DID YOU SCHEDULE YOUR BAPTISM?

When: _____

Where: _____

Who: _____

> **NOTE** Prayer is often misunderstood. Prayer is simply talking with God. Your body position (i.e. bowing your head and folding your hands) is not important. Learning how to talk to the Lord as your Father is an important next step in your faith.

Read the following and describe Jesus' prayer life:

1) *Mark 1:35 (NLT) Before daybreak the next morning, Jesus got up and went out to an isolated place to pray.*

   Matthew 14:23 (NLT) After sending them home, he went up into the hills by himself to pray. Night fell while he was there alone.

   Luke 5:16 (NLT) But Jesus often withdrew to the wilderness for prayer.

   Luke 6:12 (NLT) One day soon afterward Jesus went up on a mountain to pray, and he prayed to God all night.

   How would you describe Jesus' prayer life?

2) Hebrews 4:16 (NLT) So let us come boldly to the throne of our gracious God. There we will receive his mercy, and we will find grace to help us when we need it most.

How can we approach God and what will we receive if we do?

3) Matthew 6:6a (NLT) But when you pray, go away by yourself, shut the door behind you, and pray to your Father...

To whom do we pray?

4) John 16:24 (NLT) [Jesus said], "Ask, using my name, and you will receive, and you will have abundant joy."

In whose name (authority) do we approach the Father?

5) Romans 8:26 (NLT) And the Holy Spirit helps us in our weakness. For example, we don't know what God wants us to pray for. But the Holy Spirit prays for us with groanings that cannot be expressed in words.

Who helps us pray?

NOTE We pray to the Father, in the authority of the Son, as the Holy Spirit helps us.

6) Philippians 4:6b-7 (NLT) pray about everything. Tell God what you need, and thank him for all he has done. [7] Then you will experience God's peace, which exceeds anything we can understand. His peace will guard your hearts and minds as you live in Christ Jesus.

What will you experience if you pray instead of worrying?

☐ THE DISCIPLES ASKED JESUS, "LORD, TEACH US TO PRAY." HERE IS WHAT HE TAUGHT THEM:

Our Father in heaven, Hallowed be Your name. Your kingdom come. Your will be done On earth as it is in heaven. Give us this day our daily bread. And forgive us our debts, As we forgive our debtors. And do not lead us into temptation, But deliver us from the evil one. For Yours is the kingdom and the power and the glory forever. Amen. Matthew 6:9-13 (NKJV)

With a partner, work your way through this prayer one phrase at a time until you know how to pray using this prayer as a guide:

Phrase	Meaning
Our Father in heaven	Jesus taught us to pray to God as our Father. You can even call Him, "Dad" or "Daddy" or "Papa."
Hallowed be Your name	Begin your prayers by praising and thanking the Lord. Think of specific things for which you can be thankful.
Your kingdom come	Pray for the people in your life who are far from God.
Your will be done on earth as it is in heaven	Pray for the areas in your life where you are struggling to obey God. Ask God to help you obey Him.
Give us this day our daily bread.	Tell God your needs: physical, financial, emotional, relationship and spiritual needs.
And forgive us our debts (sins)	Confess your sins to the Lord. Thank Him for the forgiveness He has provided through Jesus.
As we forgive our debtors (those who have sinned against us).	Ask the Lord to help you forgive those who have hurt you.
And do not lead us into temptation, But deliver us from the evil one.	Ask the Lord to lead you away from temptation and to protect you from the evil one and his lies.
For Yours is the kingdom and the power and the glory forever.	End your prayer by praising the Lord for all He has done for you.
Amen.	The word Amen means "may it be so."

7) **Hebrews 11:6a (NLT) And it is impossible to please God without faith.**

What attitude should we have when we pray?

8) **Psalm 66:18 (NLT) If I had not confessed the sin in my heart, the Lord would not have listened.**

What hinders God answering your prayers?

9) **1 John 5:14–15 (NIV84) This is the confidence we have in approaching God: that if we ask anything according to his will, he hears us. [15] And if we know that he hears us— whatever we ask—we know that we have what we asked of him.**

When does God give you what you ask for?

ASSIGNMENT FOR NEXT TIME:

1. Continuing reading the Gospel of John. Read it more than once.

2. Spend time each day in prayer. Pray through the Lord's Prayer the way you have learned today.

MEMORIZE

> *Philippians 4:6–7 (NLT) Don't worry about anything; instead, pray about everything. Tell God what you need, and thank him for all he has done. Then you will experience God's peace, which exceeds anything we can understand. His peace will guard your hearts and minds as you live in Christ Jesus.*

☐ CLOSE IN PRAYER TOGETHER

Session 4—Bible Study & Devotions

☐ BEGIN BY PRAYING TOGETHER

☐ LIST A HIGHLIGHT FROM LAST WEEK & CHALLENGE YOU ARE FACING

Highlight	Challenge
_____	_____
_____	_____

☐ HOW ARE YOU DOING READING THE GOSPEL OF JOHN?

☐ DID YOU SPEND TIME PRAYING THIS PAST WEEK? TELL ME ABOUT IT.

☐ DID YOU MEMORIZE PHILIPPIANS 4:6-7? IF SO, CAN YOU SHARE IT?

☐ SHOW THE NEW DISCIPLE HOW TO USE YOUVERSION BIBLE APP

We would encourage you to download the free
YouVersion Bible App, which can be a valuable
resource to you as you read and study the Bible.

YouVersion

> **NOTE**
> There are many different Bibles. We would suggest that you use either a New International Version (NIV) or the New Living Translation (NLT). For serious Bible study we would recommend the ESV Study Bible, which contains notes, explanations and outlines to help you understand the Bible.

☐ IN EACH OF THE NEXT 4 PASSAGES CIRCLE OR UNDERLINE A BENEFIT FOR STUDYING THE BIBLE:

1) *Psalm 1:1–3 (NLT) Oh, the joys of those who do not follow the advice of the wicked, or stand around with sinners, or join in with mockers. [2] But they delight in the law of the LORD, meditating on it day and night. [3] They are like trees planted along the riverbank, bearing fruit each season. Their leaves never wither, and they prosper in all they do.*

12

2) *Romans 15:4 (NLT) Such things were written in the Scriptures long ago to teach us. And the Scriptures give us hope and encouragement as we wait patiently for God's promises to be fulfilled.*

3) *Psalm 19:8 (NLT) The commandments of the LORD are right, bringing joy to the heart. The commands of the LORD are clear, giving insight for living.*

4) *James 1:22, 25 (NLT) But don't just listen to God's word. You must do what it says. Otherwise, you are only fooling yourselves...*[25]* But if you look carefully into the perfect law that sets you free, and if you do what it says and don't forget what you heard, then God will bless you for doing it.*

****

5) *Psalm 42:1–2 (NLT) As the deer longs for streams of water, so I long for you, O God. I thirst for God, the living God. When can I go and stand before him?*

How should you feel about spending time with God?

6) *Psalm 119:147–148 (NLT) I rise early, before the sun is up; I cry out for help and put my hope in your words. I stay awake through the night, thinking about your promise.*

What priority should you give to studying the Bible?

☐ HOW TO STUDY THE BIBLE: 3 QUESTIONS FOR STUDYING GOD'S WORD

NOTE
Carefully read a section of the Bible (it could be a chapter or a couple of paragraphs). Then write out your answer to these 3 questions (below). Practice with the following Bible story. Read this story then answer the 3 questions.

7) *Luke 5:17–26 (NLT) One day while Jesus was teaching, some Pharisees and teachers of religious law were sitting nearby. (It seemed that these men showed up from every village in all Galilee and Judea, as well as from Jerusalem.) And the Lord's healing power was strongly with Jesus. [18] Some men came carrying a paralyzed man on a sleeping mat. They tried to take him inside to Jesus, [19] but they couldn't reach him because of the crowd. So they went up to the roof and took off some tiles. Then they lowered the sick man on his mat down into the crowd, right in front of Jesus. [20] Seeing their faith, Jesus said to the man, "Young man, your sins are forgiven." [21] But the Pharisees and teachers of religious law said to themselves, "Who does he think he is? That's blasphemy! Only God can forgive sins!" [22] Jesus knew what they were thinking, so he asked them, "Why do you question this in your hearts? [23] Is it easier to say 'Your sins are forgiven,' or 'Stand up and walk'? [24] So I will prove to you that the Son of Man has the authority on earth to forgive sins." Then Jesus turned to the paralyzed man and said, "Stand up, pick up your mat, and go home!" [25] And immediately, as everyone watched, the man jumped up, picked up his mat, and went home praising God. [26] Everyone was gripped with great wonder and awe, and they praised God, exclaiming, "We have seen amazing things today!"*

#1. What is something interesting you notice about this passage?

#2. What is a question you have about what you read or something you don't understand?

#3. What is something God would have you do (obey) as a result of this Bible passage?

NOTE Use these 3 questions to study any Bible passage.

☐ DAILY TIME WITH GOD—YOUR COMMITMENT

The content of our Daily Devotions
- o Talk with God through prayer
- o Let God speak to me through reading the Bible

The purpose of our Daily Devotions
- o To worship God – God welcomes me
- o To develop friendship with God – I share my concerns
- o To be led by God – I ask God to guide my life

Are you willing to commit to a Daily Devotion? ☐ Yes   ☐ No Signature_____ • Beginning date: _____ • Time or Times of Day: _____ • Place:_____ Below, describe your Daily Devotion plan. What books will you read? How will you pray?

ASSIGNMENT FOR NEXT TIME:

1. After you have finished the Gospel of John by reading it through at least twice, begin to read the book of Philippians.

2. Spend daily time with God doing your devotions (praying and reading the Bible—use the 3 questions as you read)

MEMORIZE

Job 23:12 (NIV84) I have not departed from the commands of his lips; I have treasured the words of his mouth more than my daily bread.

☐ CLOSE IN PRAYER TOGETHER

Session 5—Your Faith Story

☐ BEGIN BY PRAYING TOGETHER

☐ LIST A HIGHLIGHT FROM LAST WEEK & CHALLENGE YOU ARE FACING

Highlight   Challenge

_____   _____

_____   _____

☐ HOW ARE YOU DOING WITH YOUR DAILY DEVOTIONS?

☐ DID YOU MEMORIZE JOB 23:12? IF SO, CAN YOU SHARE IT?

> **NOTE**
> Since becoming a Christian, (or becoming recommitted to your faith) you have developed a greater assurance that you have eternal life; you have followed Jesus command by being baptized; you have grown in your communication with God through prayer and Bible study. Now it is time to begin sharing what you're learning with others.

Question 1: Why should I tell others about Jesus?

1) *1 Peter 3:15–16a (NLT) Instead, you must worship Christ as Lord of your life. And if someone asks about your Christian hope, always be ready to explain it. But do this in a gentle and respectful way.*

   What does God want you to be ready to do?

   Are you ready to explain your Christian hope to someone?

2) *Matthew 28:19–20 (NLT) "Therefore, go and make disciples of all the nations, baptizing them in the name of the Father and the Son and the Holy Spirit. Teach these new disciples to obey all the commands I have given you. And be sure of this: I am with you always, even to the end of the age."*

   Why should you tell people about Jesus?

3) *2 Corinthians 5:17–18 (NLT) This means that anyone who belongs to Christ has become a new person. The old life is gone; a new life has begun! And all of this is a gift from God, who brought us back to himself through Christ. And God has given us this task of reconciling people to him.*

What task has God given to us to do?

4) *2 Corinthians 5:20 (NLT) So we are Christ's ambassadors; God is making his appeal through us. We speak for Christ when we plead, "Come back to God!"*

We are Christ's ambassadors. What does an Ambassador do?

Question 2: Who should I tell about Jesus?

5) *Mark 5:18–19 (NLT) As Jesus was getting into the boat, the man who had been demon possessed begged to go with him. [19] But Jesus said, "No, go home to your family, and tell them everything the Lord has done for you and how merciful he has been."*

What did Jesus tell this new Christian to do?

6) *Acts 10:24 (NLT) They arrived in Caesarea the following day. Cornelius was waiting for them and had called together his relatives and close friends.*

Who did Cornelius want to hear about Jesus?

7) *Acts 16:14–15a (NLT) One of them was Lydia from Thyatira, a merchant of expensive purple cloth, who worshiped God. As she listened to us, the Lord opened her heart, and she accepted what Paul was saying. She was baptized along with other members of her household...*

Who believed in Jesus in this passage?

8) Acts 16:30–32 (NLT) *Then he brought them out and asked, "Sirs, what must I do to be saved?"* [31] *They replied, "Believe in the Lord Jesus and you will be saved, along with everyone in your household."* [32] *And they shared the word of the Lord with him and with all who lived in his household.*

Who heard about and believed in Jesus in this story?

WHO ARE THE PEOPLE IN YOUR LIFE WHO NEED TO HEAR ABOUT JESUS?

NAME LIST

List the names of people in your family, extended family, closest friends and associates who need to know Jesus as their Savior.

_____	_____
_____	_____
_____	_____
_____	_____
_____	_____
_____	_____
_____	_____
_____	_____
_____	_____
_____	_____
_____	_____

NOTE — Don't stress out about telling the people on your list about Jesus. For now simply list their names and pray for them often. God will provide you with opportunities to talk with them about spiritual things.

Question 3: How should I tell about Jesus?

Answer: Write Your Faith Story

1. What word would you choose to characterize your life before you began seriously following Jesus (or before God intervened in your life during a difficult time)?

My word:

Now write 2 or 3 sentences of explanation to describe this in more detail.

2. Write 2 or 3 sentences to describe what happened when you began seriously following Jesus (or how God intervened in your life). Provide a few details of what you experienced, what you were feeling, etc.

3. What word would you choose to describe how knowing Jesus makes you feel?

My word:

Now explain this in more detail in 2 or 3 sentences. You are describing the benefits of being a Christian.

Additional Room to Write...

ASSIGNMENT FOR NEXT TIME:

1. Continue your Daily Devotions.

2. Pray for the names on your Name List every day that they will come to know Jesus. You may want to put them in a note on your phone so you have your list with you at all times.

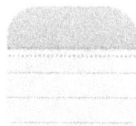

Notes

3. Finish writing Your Faith Story and bring it with you next time.

MEMORIZE

1 Peter 3:15–16a (NLT) Instead, you must worship Christ as Lord of your life. And if someone asks about your Christian hope, always be ready to explain it. But do this in a gentle and respectful way.

☐   CLOSE IN PRAYER TOGETHER

Session 6—God's Story

□ BEGIN BY PRAYING TOGETHER

□ LIST A HIGHLIGHT FROM LAST WEEK & CHALLENGE YOU ARE FACING

Highlight	Challenge
_____	_____
_____	_____

□ DID YOU FINISHING WRITING YOUR FAITH STORY? IF SO, SHARE IT.

□ ARE YOU STAYING CONSISTENT WITH YOUR DAILY DEVOTIONS?

□ HAVE YOU BEEN PRAYING FOR THE PEOPLE ON YOUR NAME LIST?

□ DID YOU MEMORIZE 1 PETER 3:15-16? IF SO, CAN YOU SHARE IT?

> **NOTE**
> Once you are able to share **Your Story** (Faith Story), you then should learn to share **God's Story**, which is a simple explanation of the Gospel (Good News). We call this THE BRIDGE. Whenever you share Your Story always share God's Story using THE BRIDGE.

1) *Romans 1:16 (NLT) For I am not ashamed of this Good News about Christ. It is the power of God at work, saving everyone who believes—the Jew first and also the Gentile.*

   Are you ashamed of the Good News about Jesus?

2) *Ephesians 6:19–20 (NIV84) Pray also for me, that whenever I open my mouth, words may be given me so that I will fearlessly make known the mystery of the gospel, for which I am an ambassador in chains. Pray that I may declare it fearlessly, as I should.*

   What should you pray for according to this verse?

THE BRIDGE

INSTRUCTIONS:	YOU SAY:
Have a piece of paper ready and begin...	Let me share how you can be sure you have Eternal Life... In the book of Romans chapter 6, verse 23, it says, "**For the wages of sin is death, but the gift of God is eternal life in Christ Jesus our Lord.**"
Draw lines to indicate a great canyon between God and man. Draw a stick-man on one side and write "God" on the other.	People are separated from God because of sin. It is as if we were on one side, and God was on the other side of a great canyon. What separates us from God is our sin. People have tried many ways to bridge the gap between themselves and God. They have tried good deeds, philosophy, even religion, but all of our efforts to bridge the gap fall short.
As you say it, write "wages," "sin," and "death" under the man.	The Bible says that what we have earned (**wages**) for being a sinner (**sin**) is death (**death**). Death means more than just physical death—it means separation from God.
On God's side of the canyon write "gift," and "God" and "E. L."	This verse goes on to say that a gift (**gift**) has been provided by God (**God**), and this gift is eternal life (**eternal life**). On one side of the canyon we have <u>wages</u> and <u>sin</u> and <u>death</u>. And on the other side of the canyon we have gift and God and eternal life.
Ask this question:	• **Which side of the canyon would you like to be?**
Draw an arch bridge over the canyon, then draw a cross between the two sides of the canyon.	This is where the Bridge comes in. Jesus Christ is the Bridge that God provided to give us the gift of eternal life. Through Jesus and His death on the cross to pay for our sins, we can cross over the canyon, and no longer be separated from God.
Write "Jesus" above the canyon; draw an arrow through it.	God provided the gift of eternal life in Jesus Christ. In order to cross over to God's side of the canyon, we must go through Him. He is the Bridge!
	To cross over a canyon on a bridge, you would have to trust the bridge to hold you. In the same way, in order to cross over to God, you must trust that Jesus Christ will be able to provide the way to eternal life.
Ask this question:	• **Do you trust in Jesus as your bridge to eternal life and believe that he died and rose again for your forgiveness and salvation?**
If they say, "Yes..."	Then assure them that God has worked a miracle in their heart and they have the promised gift of eternal life.
Lead them in a confession of their faith in Jesus Christ.	The Bible says, "If you confess with your mouth that Jesus is Lord and believe in your heart that God raised him from the dead, you will be saved."

Romans 6:23

Jesus →

Wages

Sin

Death

GOD

Gift

God

E. L.

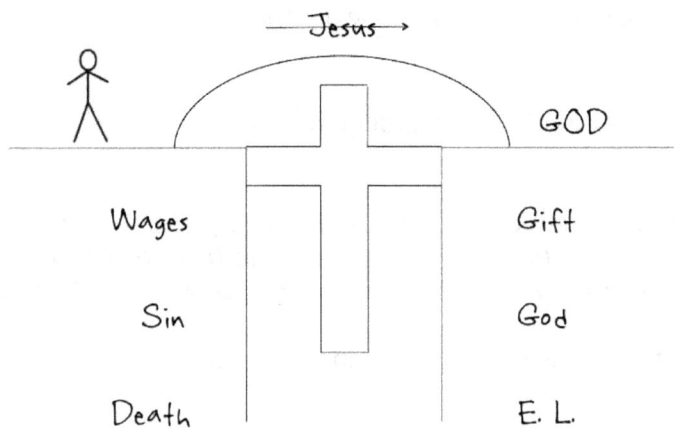

Practice drawing THE BRIDGE in the space below:

3) **John 17:3 (NIV84) Now this is eternal life: that they may know you, the only true God, and Jesus Christ, whom you have sent.**

What is Eternal Life according to Jesus?

4) **John 5:24 (NIV84) "I tell you the truth, whoever hears my word and believes him who sent me has eternal life and will not be condemned; he has crossed over from death to life."**

What happens if you believe in God who sent Jesus?

ASSIGNMENT FOR NEXT TIME:

1. Continue your Daily Devotions.

2. Continue to pray for those on your Name List.

3. Practice sharing your Faith Story whenever you have a chance.

4. Practice drawing the Bridge.

MEMORIZE

Romans 6:23 (NIV84) For the wages of sin is death, but the gift of God is eternal life in Christ Jesus our Lord.

☐ CLOSE IN PRAYER TOGETHER

Session 7—Church: Christian Community

☐ BEGIN BY PRAYING TOGETHER

☐ LIST A HIGHLIGHT FROM LAST WEEK & CHALLENGE YOU ARE FACING

Highlight   Challenge

_____   _____

_____   _____

☐ ARE YOU STAYING CONSISTENT WITH YOUR DAILY DEVOTIONS?

☐ HAVE YOU BEEN PRAYING FOR THE PEOPLE ON YOUR NAME LIST?

☐ DID YOU SHARE THE BRIDGE AND EXPLAIN IT TO ANYONE? WHO?

☐ DID YOU MEMORIZE ROMANS 6:23? IF SO, CAN YOU SHARE IT?

> **NOTE**
>
> When you become a Christian, you are a member of God's family. God is your heavenly Father, and all Christians are like brothers and sisters of the same family, *"...this household is the church of the living God..." (I Timothy 3:15)*. The "church" is not a building, and the "church" is not a place of worship, but it is a body (a connected gathering) of believers in a family-like unit.

1) *"You should be like one big happy family, full of sympathy toward each other, loving one another with tender hearts and humble minds."* (1 Peter 3:8, LB)

How should we think of our other believers?

2) *Hebrews 10:24–25 (NLT) Let us think of ways to motivate one another to acts of love and good works. [25] And let us not neglect our meeting together, as some people do, but encourage one another, especially now that the day of his return is drawing near.*

Why is it important to meet together as the church?

3) *Acts 2:41–47 (NLT) Those who believed what Peter said were baptized and added to the church that day—about 3,000 in all. [42] All the believers devoted themselves to the apostles' teaching, and to fellowship, and to sharing in meals (including the Lord's Supper), and to prayer. [43] A deep sense of awe came over them all, and the apostles performed many miraculous signs and wonders. [44] And all the believers met together in one place and shared everything they had. [45] They sold their property and possessions and shared the money with those in need. [46] They worshiped together at the Temple each day, met in homes for the Lord's Supper, and shared their meals with great joy and generosity—[47] all the while praising God and enjoying the goodwill of all the people. And each day the Lord added to their fellowship those who were being saved.*

Find and circle each practice listed below in the above passage:

- ☐ Baptism
- ☐ Care for each other
- ☐ Worship
- ☐ Learn the Bible
- ☐ Giving
- ☐ Make Disciples
- ☐ Lord's Supper
- ☐ Prayer
- ☐ Qualified Leaders

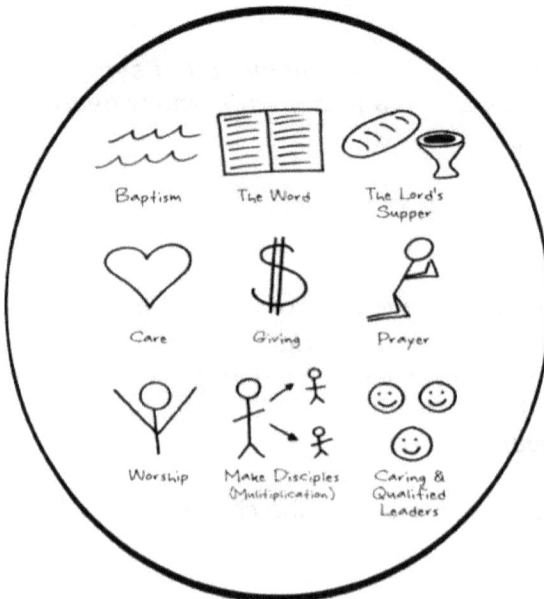

Baptism The Word The Lord's Supper

Care Giving Prayer

Worship Make Disciples (Multiplication) Caring & Qualified Leaders

Who is your church?
The question is not, "Where do you go to church?" but rather, "Who is your church?" Who are the people with whom you are being the church?

We practice these 9 things as we grow in our faith together. This is what the church is supposed to do. You have already learned about some of these in previous Sessions: You have learned how to care for each other. In Session 2 Baptism was explained, in Session 3 Prayer, Session 4 Bible Study, and in Sessions 5 & 6 you were taught how to Make Disciples.

But there are 3 practices that may need further explanation:

UNDERSTANDING FINANCIAL GIVING

4) **2 Corinthians 9:6-7 (NLT) "Remember this -- a farmer who plants only a few seeds will get a small crop. But the one who plants generously will get a generous crop. You must each make up your own mind as to how much you should give. Don't give reluctantly or in response to pressure. For God loves the person who gives cheerfully."**

What does the Bible teach about our financial giving?

UNDERSTANDING THE LORD'S SUPPER

5) **1 Corinthians 11:23–26 (NLT) For I pass on to you what I received from the Lord himself. On the night when he was betrayed, the Lord Jesus took some bread [24] and gave thanks to God for it. Then he broke it in pieces and said, "This is my body, which is given for you. Do this to remember me." [25] In the same way, he took the cup of wine after supper, saying, "This cup is the new covenant between God and his people—an agreement confirmed with my blood. Do this to remember me as often as you drink it." [26] For every time you eat this bread and drink this cup, you are announcing the Lord's death until he comes again.**

What are the 4 elements you receive in the Lord's Supper?

What benefits are received in the Lord's Supper?

What is the purpose of the Lord's Supper?

When and where can you share the Lord's Supper with other Christians?

27

UNDERSTANDING QUALIFIED LEADERS: God has provided order in the church by equipping leaders to lead His people.

6) *Hebrews 13:17 (NLT) Obey your spiritual leaders, and do what they say. Their work is to watch over your souls, and they are accountable to God. Give them reason to do this with joy and not with sorrow. That would certainly not be for your benefit.*

What does this passage say about the leaders, and your response to them? Who are those leaders for you?

> **NOTE** Next week you will experience church in a small group setting. You and your leader will arrange to meet with a small group of Christian friends to practice being the church.

ASSIGNMENT FOR NEXT TIME:

1. Continue your Daily Devotions.

2. Continue to pray for those on your Name List and share your Faith Story and THE BRIDGE whenever you have an opportunity.

3. Plan a small group meeting with some friends so that you can practice being the church.

4. Begin thinking about who you could lead through this study.

> **MEMORIZE** *Hebrews 10:24–25 (NLT) Let us think of ways to motivate one another to acts of love and good works. And let us not neglect our meeting together, as some people do, but encourage one another, especially now that the day of his return is drawing near.*

□ CLOSE IN PRAYER TOGETHER

Session 8—Practice Being the Church

NOTE This Session must be done with a small group of other Christians. It can be as few as 3 or 4, or could be many more. You are encouraged to begin with sharing a meal together if possible.

Explain that you are going to practice these 9 things together:

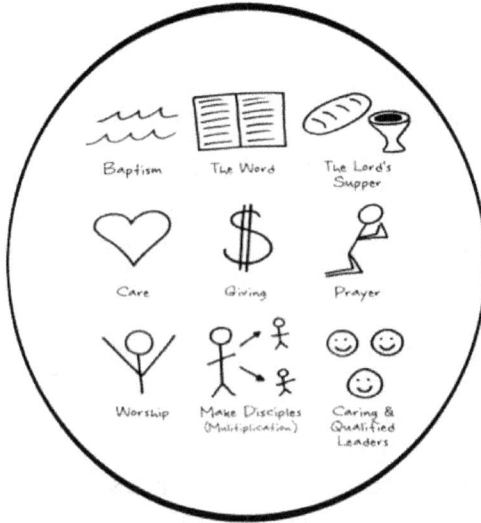

If you have had a meal together, begin this program after your meal.

You may wish to assign each part of this program ahead of time, or ask for volunteers for each part.

I. PRAY TOGETHER:
   a. Begin with an opening prayer
   b. Have someone volunteer to pray

II. WORSHIP TOGETHER:
   a. Read a Psalm or other Scripture... or...
   b. Sing along with a worship video

III. CARE FOR EACH OTHER:
   a. Each person share a highlight from last week
   b. Each person share a challenge they are currently facing

IV. MAKE DISCIPLES & BAPTISM
   a. Pray for the names on your Name List
   b. Share people you are talking to about the Lord
   c. Ask if anyone needs to be baptized

V. SHARE THE LORD'S SUPPER TOGETHER. Read this Bible passage:

Matthew 26:26–28 (NLT) As they were eating, Jesus took some bread and blessed it. Then he broke it in pieces and gave it to the disciples, saying, "Take this and eat it, for this is my body." [27] And he took a cup of wine and gave thanks to God for it. He gave it to them and said, "Each of you drink from it, [28] for this is my blood, which confirms the covenant between God and his people. It is poured out as a sacrifice to forgive the sins of many."

Discuss an appropriate place and time to share the Lord's Supper together. Plan to do this, after consulting your church leaders.

VI. GIVING—discuss a Christian charity, project, or church you would like to support. Receive an offering from your group members and make sure it gets to the right place. No one should feel obligated to give.

VII. BIBLE LESSON—Read and discuss these "Each Other" Bible passages which teach us how to interact with one another as Christians. Ask: How will you obey what you are learning?

1) *Romans 15:7 (NLT) Therefore, accept each other just as Christ has accepted you so that God will be given glory.*

2) *1 Corinthians 1:10 (NLT) I appeal to you, dear brothers and sisters, by the authority of our Lord Jesus Christ, to live in harmony with each other. Let there be no divisions in the church. Rather, be of one mind, united in thought and purpose.*

3) *Colossians 3:13 (NLT) Make allowance for each other's faults, and forgive anyone who offends you. Remember, the Lord forgave you, so you must forgive others.*

4) *1 Thessalonians 5:11 (NLT) So encourage each other and build each other up, just as you are already doing.*

5) *Galatians 6:2 (NLT) Share each other's burdens, and in this way obey the law of Christ.*

6) *James 5:16 (NLT) Confess your sins to each other and pray for each other so that you may be healed. The earnest prayer of a righteous person has great power and produces wonderful results.*

7) *1 Peter 3:8 (NLT) Finally, all of you should be of one mind. Sympathize with each other. Love each other as brothers and sisters. Be tenderhearted, and keep a humble attitude.*

8) *1 Peter 4:9 (NIV) Offer hospitality to one another without grumbling.*

9) *1 Peter 5:5b (NLT) And all of you, serve each other in humility, for "God opposes the proud but favors the humble."*

10) *John 13:35 (NLT) "Your love for one another will prove to the world that you are my disciples."*

VIII. OBEY—Each person shares which of these Scriptures they will put into practice this coming week and how they will do it.

ASSIGNMENT FOR NEXT TIME:

NEXT STEPS—Ask: **"What if we met together once a week a few times and we studied an overview of the entire Bible?"**
o Show THRU THE BIBLE study booklet.
o Ask for commitment: What do you think?
o Schedule time & date for your next meeting.

NOTE

IX. PRAY TOGETHER—close in prayer.

MEMORIZE

John 13:35 (NLT) "Your love for one another will prove to the world that you are my disciples."

MEMORY VERSES

Session 1 *Romans 10:9 (NLT) If you confess with your mouth that Jesus is Lord and believe in your heart that God raised him from the dead, you will be saved.*	**Session 5** *1 Peter 3:15–16a (NLT) Instead, you must worship Christ as Lord of your life. And if someone asks about your Christian hope, always be ready to explain it. But do this in a gentle and respectful way.*
Session 2 *Acts 22:16 (NLT) What are you waiting for? Get up and be baptized. Have your sins washed away by calling on the name of the Lord.'*	**Session 6** *Romans 6:23 (NIV84) For the wages of sin is death, but the gift of God is eternal life in Christ Jesus our Lord.*
Session 3 *Philippians 4:6–7 (NLT) Don't worry about anything; instead, pray about everything. Tell God what you need, and thank him for all he has done. ⁷ Then you will experience God's peace, which exceeds anything we can understand. His peace will guard your hearts and minds as you live in Christ Jesus.*	**Session 7** *Hebrews 10:24–25 (NLT) Let us think of ways to motivate one another to acts of love and good works. ²⁵ And let us not neglect our meeting together, as some people do, but encourage one another, especially now that the day of his return is drawing near.*
Session 4 *Job 23:12 (NIV84) I have not departed from the commands of his lips; I have treasured the words of his mouth more than my daily bread.*	**Session 8** *John 13:35 (NLT) "Your love for one another will prove to the world that you are my disciples."*

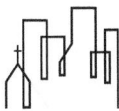

TRANSFORMING
CHURCHES NETWORK

Transforming Churches Network
1736 Edgeburg Lane
Cordova, TN 38016
901-494-7375
www.tcnprocess.com
terry@transformingchurchesnetwork.org

www.ingramcontent.com/pod-product-compliance
Lightning Source LLC
Chambersburg PA
CBHW071941020426
42331CB00010B/2970